SALT WATE

Jeffrey Skinner

AUSABLE PRESS
2005

Cover art:
Gregory D. West, "High and Dry"
oil on canvas, 40" x 24"

Design and composition by Ausable Press
The type is Granjon with Felix Titling.
Cover design by Rebecca Soderholm

Published by
AUSABLE PRESS
1026 HURRICANE ROAD
KEENE, NY 12942
www.ausablepress.org

Distributed to the trade by
CONSORTIUM BOOK SALES & DISTRIBUTION
1045 WESTGATE DRIVE
SAINT PAUL, MN 55114-1065
(651) 221-9035
(651) 221-0124 (FAX)
(800) 283-3572 (ORDERS)

The acknowledgments appear on page 81 and constititute a
continuation of the copyright page.

First Edition

Library of Congress Cataloging-in-Publication Data

Skinner, Jeffrey.
Salt water amnesia / Jeffrey Skinner.
p. cm.
ISBN 978-1-931337-25-0
I. Title.

PS3569.K498S25 2005
811'.54—dc22
2005011203

Thomas Franklin Skinner, 1927—2004

"In the most intimate of my thoughts I was not myself."
                                    —*Pessoa*

"Only gradually did it dawn on me that I would never again be able to write home; in fact, to tell the truth, I do not know if I have grasped it to this day."
                                    —*Sebald*

CONTENTS

I.

WIDOW'S WALK

Flags snap inland as the water scales. Try again.
The ocean's scales point toward shore
as do the flags in offshore wind. And? Islands
on the horizon like misshapen cakes.
Days in sequence do not remake the self, only the body.
And? The ocean is the self apart from body.

One step, and another. Eyes down. If the heart
could think, it would stop. Babies see much better
and sooner than once thought. The impulse of an instant,
its deep pockets. Her goal, fist-sized: to sleep
in a pine forest with the child,
with him. Sleep, the book that reads us.

In tall marsh grass you catch the scent
of a vast unused library. Further on, the green streaked
uneven planes of coastal rock.
Wintry scales of ocean, flaked and scarred
with light. Flags like whips overhead. His ghost steps from
        the boat.
A huge hand over eyes, to find her eyes.

GULLS

The cry of a gull, very like that of a flying baby. You look up startled, walking to the quay. Wind whisks a fringe here and there on the sound's surface, which from a distance you may confuse with gulls, their wings out and resting on a wave's lip. The difficulty of starting the whole machinery up, over and over—waking in the morning, brushing teeth, making the bed, slicing a banana for the cereal . . . The even odder thing called writing, which is not work exactly, nor play, nor worship, nor a waste of time. Not exactly. Gulls follow the boat home, turning in a great circle like a paddlewheel off the stern, not for scraps thrown by sentimental fisherman (none exist) but for flashes churned to the wake's surface by the boat's plow through water. It occurs to me that all gulls have been ruined forever by that stupid book. You know the one. Words *can* impair vision. But it's all right: everyone who read it will soon enough be gone, the book gone. New people will see gulls again, each one itself, skiing the air without precedent. The flight of a gull: a skiing in three dimensions. Like speed chess on a three tiered board. Occasionally one sees a gull who has lost a leg, walking like a stick, begging for scraps at the pier. *Don't want sympathy, want fish.* Lastly, I wonder whether fishermen even see or hear gulls at all. If, in time, gulls become for them like those people in the office, with whom you exchange only necessities of word and gesture. If the journey, restless and foreshortened by waves, is the same for gull and fisherman: port to sea, back: work between.

MANY WORLDS

A physicist proposes time does not exist, only an infinite number of dramas, grand or banal, in different locations: a Wyoming ant hefts a leaf and begins the blind trek home. Nancy nicks her thumb chopping arugula in Manhattan. Sheets of rain batter the empty head of a seagull hunkered down amid blonde grasses. A Sudanese teenager takes the first of nineteen steps toward a landmine he will, or will not, trip with his left foot. A star in a tri-folded galaxy sputters and implodes. And so forth, ad infinitum. I read about this while drinking a steaming hot Columbian blend on the day we call, for convenience sake, Sunday.

But if there is no time, I wonder as I take another sip, why do I keep needing stronger glasses? And, if time is to be summarily tossed onto some landfill, wouldn't we be wise to hire a caretaker, an experienced force to guard the perimeter? One would not want the Spanish Inquisition leaking into Stonington, for example, where I currently reside. And I do not like to imagine walking the frozen streets of Buffalo, New York, and bumping into myself at the age of two, bundled in my mother's arms as she hurries me into the hospital, my appendix burst, my time running out.

How immediately I bend the poor physicist's notion to my own fears and wishes . . . Why must I understand every idea in terms of myself, my own little life and death? In all probability I misunderstand him completely and do not, as usual, know what I'm talking about. I wish I could step outside, into one of the many worlds to the left and right of me. *The boy recovered, in time, and lived.* But if time does not exist then why, as I continue sipping, does my sorrow deepen?

SKY CAPS

This morning when I looked out the window I was once again surprised by the ocean. That's what I get for living so long in the Midwest. The absence of salt water: a kind of amnesia. In this new place, right next to the ocean, *of course* the window fills with waves.

Today the weather is blowy, the waves have those frilly things on the tops. I want to call them skycaps, but that's not right; I'm thinking of the men who check your luggage at the airport. But many things *will* return to me, I am convinced, in the course of my hiatus by the sea.

Excuse me for a moment, while I pound my head against the wall . . . Ah, that's better: Whitecaps. Whitecaps hurry the gray luggage of the sea to shore. *Be sure your ticket matches,* I now remember the sky caps telling me, time after time: *Many waves look similar to your own.*

THE LONG MARRIAGE

They could not believe their luck—sunlight all the way down, lighting rocks lodged in the sandy bottom as if from within. Each rock angled just so, by some immense but casual intelligence. Rock weed held out its dark green fingers, waving. How can the water be so clear, and full of salt? In between their visits someone had removed the used condoms and shattered beer glass from the concrete cubicles, the breakwater fronting the old factory. *The olfactory,* he said. She did not see the humor.

At the beach a group gathered around the harbor seal who had hauled herself a small way onto the shore, waving an aristocratic flipper in the sun. Can't a mammal have a bit of privacy? She knew the feeling. The vertebra he plucked from the sand and showed her proudly was smooth, and cleanest white. But she would not have it in the house. Be happy you are alive and moving, she said. Bones belong in sand, rocks on ocean floor, and mercy in the great, shadowy hands of the indifferent one.

LETTER TO PESSOA

We still dream of going to a new city, leaving the old self behind. Sometimes we do. Recently, when a group of friends disappeared, the old selves they left behind decided to get together for coffee. One ordered a skinny latte, one a mocha grande, one a coffee of the day. Just like their absent masters. Then they chatted about last night's basketball game, and the front moving in from Canada. At one point Latte punched Mocha's shoulder, gently teasing him. Gradually they forgot their abandonment and began to think of getting to work. Coffee of the day, the woman of the trio, left first. The two men watched her ass as she walked off, then pretended they had not. Then they themselves got up and went to work.

The place I am spending my sabbatical is nice. The ocean borders the town on three sides and the sun rises in the windows on one side of the house and sets in the windows on the other. It is just as I remember it from Jones Beach in 1958. "You don't look a day older than the last time I saw you!" I even said to the water. And it didn't. I'm getting work done and everyone I love is ok. Can't say I miss *you,* since you died in 1935 and obviously we never met. Except in *The Book of Disquiet,* where I wander a little each morning. Five feet seven, one hundred and twenty-four pounds: You were one luminous tightly-folded heartbreaking newborn genius, Fernando.

Meanwhile the three originals, lying on a beach in Antigua. Silence. Coffee of the day, wearing a two-piece, stretched out on a chaise in the middle. Latte and Mocha on either side. All three wear sunglasses and their skin, turning a lovely shade of dark roasted Sumatra with cream, glistens and winks in the sun. They sleep, and dream again the old dream of leaving. Later that night they will gamble and drink. Later still, so late it begins to be early, the three will go back to the hotel and do things to each other they could never have imagined in their other life. They will go too far. They will not come back. Wait. Perhaps we have met. But what sea, which universe, old friend?

THAT NOBODY THING

I was in a car with David Letterman when he quite unexpectedly proposed marriage. He did it in that offhand, ironic, deadpan, winning way of his, but I could see that he was serious. "Well, all right, I guess." I said. "But," I added in afterthought, "I'm not gay, and I didn't think you were either." David took a puff of his cigar and assured me that he was not gay, and that he chose me partially because I *wasn't* gay. And *that,* he said, his voice rising excitedly, was the beauty of it! When the news was released, the media would surely portray us as pioneering heros: two men who, even though straight, chose to marry each other. The show's ratings would go through the roof. David would suddenly become the most admired celebrity in the world, immune to criticism. And the fact that he was marrying, not a Hollywood type, but a nobody, would only add to his luster. Here he turned to me and apologized, "For that nobody thing—Sorry." I told him it was all right, I *was* a nobody.

We were stopped at a light, and when I looked around I saw that all the other cars were being driven by animals of some kind—a moose eyed me morosely from the wheel of a Hummer to our right, an Emperor Penguin stood upright in the PT Cruiser windshield behind us, and so on. "David," I began, hesitantly. "Will we . . . will we sleep in the same bed?" There was a horrible screech as tires gnawed asphalt and David wove, needle-like, through traffic, finally lurching to a halt amid dust and flung gravel on the shoulder. He turned his large, red face to me. "Don't you *ever,*" he said, "speak such filth in my car, my beautiful car, again." "Ok, ok, ok," I said. "Take a chill pill, Jeeze." Back in the flow of traffic it was very quiet, and I had time to meditate on several pressing issues, such as: Had I been wrong to say yes so quickly? And: This universe is strange and fleeting, but is it really that much more so than the one I call my real life? And: That orangutan, the one in the silver Jetta, did he or did he not just give us the finger?

THE COLT

In the field and everywhere I am never far from mother.
Mother covers my face with her tail and the brightness of sky
is split. When there is danger mother puts her body
between me and danger. In the center of the field an island
of trees fenced in. Why an island of trees fenced in?
Sometimes I must rear up suddenly in the wind
and run, fast, so that all my mind is running
and then I don't care about danger and I am glad
for the fence or else I would never stop. Tired now
of maintaining this poem in the voice of a young horse
I rise and walk out: enormous brain, wobbling on toothpicks.

MY DATES

On a long beach walk in winter I transcended my envy. The cold white spray of breakers starched it out. By the time I reached the rocky point of Misquamicut I could think of no one with whom I would trade fortunes. In fact I did not think, only sat on a boulder below the tide line and looked down at surf slapping the boulder's hard skirt, as if the ocean might climb up and convert me to the Church of Holy Liquidity. I was beautifully inhuman, and don't remember the feel of my own body. The ocean's single-minded dedication made sense, tumbling smooth and small the rocks and wood and hunks of glass. Dead life too was converted, into darting bodies, rubbery shapes. The sea: professional, gray, unhurried. Heavy as lead one day, translucent lime floating beneath the air the next.

The bad news: I began to envy the ocean, which I realized had already outlived me countless times, and in all those lifetimes never stopped coming, violent and fresh as birth, slamming down without discrimination on the grit or rock-plane shore, wood glass rock or bone. It seemed to have both immortal soul *and* body. It buried its dead and then began the resurrection at once—same place, same time. From the beginning humans came to worship the waves and the sea's stubborn indifference to beauty. As I walked, I gradually regained the hard borders of human form. When I got home everything was the same. I was again afraid of death, or rather, afraid of the immensities that lay on either side of my consciousness: my dates, separated by a dash. The dash, unmoving.

WHITE DWARF

One day when our sun runs out of fuel and collapses inward under its own weight, then picks up enough mass from its neighbor to explode outward, the blown debris approaching a good fraction of the speed of light, then, then you'll be sorry. Oh, relax: we have five billion years, give or take a few million, to prepare. Meanwhile we go on believing the universe has our best interests at heart. The dock down at Groton Long Point throws a lovely wood skeleton fifty yards out into the Sound. There we rest, after a bike ride, and the winds rise by our witness and the waves build, and the paper-white sails and hulls of pleasure boats cut scimitars into the bay. We sit close-pressed and watch without speaking, wanting to live here, in this model galaxy of islands and peninsulas and rock borders where earth, water and air meet in the small fires of our blood. Oh, why not. We watch a long time. I whisper to you. It is the middle of the day but your hair has that scrubbed protein smell once locked in the center of a star. *Why not here?* This is what I whisper. Even as we speak, close galaxies are speeding away, faster than more distant galaxies, which are also receding. Groton Long Point, Milky Way, heat of your body next to mine: this is where we live, now. Lovely little islands of matter, surrounded by the blank of space. And the dark taking over more real estate even as we speak. Encroaching zero of the infinite, white dwarf, my breath on your neck: even as we speak.

INDECISION

A large snake, yellow with red spots, head like a fist, emerging from a hole in the stuccoed wall. My face happens to be turned that direction, I happen to raise an eyelid at the moment the snake begins to dangle, longer and longer, toward the floor. Truth is, one simply does not want to leave sleep, and so the brain puts forward the proposal that animals are generally neutral vis à vis our existence, and this snake in particular could have no earthly interest, nor perhaps even awareness, of me, my six feet of snoring meat. But that last word is . . . a mistake, and it appears to my widening eye that the snake even now makes toward me with whippy S's across the white tile floor. He (she?) will soon be spiraling up the bedpost to join me for . . . what? A nap? A snack? It is surely time to leap up, but I don't move. Oh I must have been sleepwalking again, and during my wandering entered some kind of Zen hotel, where each room represents a different koan. I do not think that this room, this koan, is especially appropriate for me, though I admit I cannot think of an answer. And then I feel the snake's skin like smooth dry ice as he glides over my leg. I hear the jaws unhinge like the clasp of a purse, as the snake labors to fit his mouth over my head. I sense the importance of this moment, I do: how rare such opportunities in any life. And I slip back slowly into the blond meadow of sleep.

IMPATIENS IN DROUGHT

Flowering plant spread like a fan
from the window box
a hundred exhausted red faces pressing outward
immigrants from a boat stopped short
of shore by coastal agents

realize only now too late
the green tether that feeds us also
holds us back, o mirage, o my longing

NIGHT READING

A hair appeared in the poem I was reading. I brushed it aside, resumed reading. The poem, like most, would not change the world. But it was real, like a cut that heals too slowly—you can't help but look at it, closing the office door for closer inspection, wondering why the red has not run its course, whether *this* might be the locus of first erosion, your little trapdoor to mortality. The hair then reappeared. Again I brushed it away.

A third time the hair came back, calmly throwing its hair-thin shadow where it bent upward from the page, bisecting the poem's sadness, its earnest eschatology. I snatched it between thumb and forefinger, balled it into a tight dot, threw it to the floor.

Immediately the hair sprang up, and became a girl I had lusted after in eighth grade—blond, on the diving team. She was now a woman, though still dressed only in that black nylon Speedo I loved, rain or shine. She held out her hand and said, *Would you like to see what might have happened?* Sure. But when I touched her skin she turned into a threshing machine, circa 1943, the long, exposed tines glinting, somehow quaint and threatening at once.

The grit of field work in the sun gets everywhere, I'll tell you. The body's never razor clean. But I like the early dew, the day's first bronzing of the barn. And, later, the white buzz of noon, the chicken hawk's slide down sky. My sons' blond heads floating through aisles of corn. Wind, pushing grass aside as it crosses the field. My wife's long hair, undone and falling to the book she reads. This life, enough for me.

SOUVENIRS

If I hold the Empire State Building up, for example, close one eye and squint down the radio antennae, the wall of my office blurs and I see a windy place and a boy afraid of being swept up and over the steel fencing, thinking perhaps he might slow in descent as in dreams, and touch down gently in the hurrying street. But perhaps not. My friend says if a penny's dropped from this height and falls edge first to a man's head it will pass straight through his body. The man might even continue walking a few steps. Then collapse, like *this,* my friend says, crumpling abruptly to the concrete of the observation deck. The wind lifts and flutters his straight blond hair and he looks like he's falling and I laugh and crash to the deck beside him and we both laugh like hell, we can't help it. Later, on the bus ride home, he tells me he did drop a penny but couldn't see where it landed and don't tell anyone. I promise.

This and other surviving tokens I have arranged on my office shelf, my étagère.

Back on the bus the overhead light is good for one only. So your neighbor can sleep. The light of memory, dimmer still. It flickers off and on as the bus ticks over seams in the asphalt. Do I see a dead man with a penny in his shoe lying on the sidewalk in front of Radio City Music Hall? No, no . . . I am just sleeping. The light of memory is dim, and it can't be detached, not completely, from the things of this world.

ALLEGORY WITH CLOUDS, AIRPLANE AND PEACH

Lengthening out across evening sky, clouds like certain philosophies appear substantial, weighty. In fact, the child in the plane window is convinced their surface would be springy, resilient to the foot, supportive. She considers the emergency handle. Looks out again. Perhaps tunnels could be made, soft, mouse-gray excavations, burrows for sleep. A simple life, lived there—clouds as bedding and furniture, mountains and meadows. But how long would that amuse, really? The gods are petty landlords, spilling mercury from the moon across our sleeping faces . . . But now *you* are intruding again, with your own worries, your superior sense of reality. Look up. A camera-flash of sunlight off the plane's belly. Wave. The girl would find nothing in your dark theology. Better to write a childrens' book, beloved by all, and die in bed, eating a ripe peach from your lover's hand. Juice, like sunlight on your cheek. And finally it would not matter, who was the pet of whom.

THE INVALID

One of the old songs playing tag
kept inside by persistent rain
which, a billion drops striking a billion leaves
so close on each other's watery heels

sounds as one continuous
tattering rush, a waterfall surround—
and I wish, and I wish, and I wish
says the slick grass darkening, or at least

that's what the man in his skin hears
whose nurse dozes like a white fly,
who coughs, hums, continues: always, still
trying to speak for the elements.

THE COOK'S TALE

In a rare moment of repose, Achilles sat on a boulder. He was sweating, but we all were. The sun seemed very close. I sat next to him and waited a diplomatic moment before speaking. "No disrespect, General, Sir—but every time I look in on you the story's the same: Fighting, grief, more fighting, death. Your tragedy happens to you over and over, like a mechanical toy, whereas our lives feel uncertain and improvised, moment to moment. We love your story, don't get me wrong; but I wonder if *you* ever think of another life, one like ours: selling insurance, kid's education, breast cancer, a little golf on weekends . . . Of course, Your Hugeness, even as I say this I cringe with shame . . . Also, what became of your gift for music and the other arts? Should we gather that they too are a waste of time?" Achilles turned slowly to me with narrowed eyes. He was the size of at least two Iowa farm boys on the high school wrestling team. "Patroclus!" he shouted, finally. His friend came bounding over, and Achilles said, stabbing a thumb in my direction, "Who the hell is this schmo?" Patroclus shrugged. "Get him out of my sight!" And this is how I came to learn, in a previous life, the way to cook on the march, for battalions of the ravenous.

MODERN MATURITY

When I quit smoking my sense of smell increased sevenfold. I knew the drop of rain, still cloud-borne, beginning to think of its fall. Walking on the pier, I sensed the crate of marjoram and other spices nudged carelessly to the rocks, some two hundred years ago. I imagined the soft explosion of blonde dust drifting over waves . . . I can now smell my wife's moods, which has done wonders for our marriage! Last night I looked at the sky and, I swear, a clean blue-and-white burning reached me from Orion. Smells, tunneling back to childhood: thermos of coffee Mom opens on long car trips; the red-headed girl I loved because she smelled like spaghetti; the rubbery cold bathing suit; pee, chlorine . . . My hearing and eyesight are going fast, but my smell is keen as a basset hound's! In fact, I'm spending more time than ever with my basset hound, Emma. *Emma,* I say, donning my deerstalker, *Looks very like another day for the woods, what?* Oh she and I wander so happy beneath the canopy, on a trail-less floor of dry leaf, moss, stone. Everything that has ever befallen the universe, I have discovered, is written there, if only you know how to read it, and we do, my dog and I, we do.

SLEEPING IN STRANGE ROOMS

There's always an extra pillow which you bash and coax into the shape of your wife. Then, lying in the fetal position, encircle with one arm and draw close: pillow wife. You miss the scent of slightly damp hair at the base of her neck, and the way she seems to be sitting on your lap, back to chest, thigh to thigh, as you glide gently forward on your sleep swing. And there's always a sound you've never heard before, like a man's slow breathing outside the window. It takes forever to habituate. You get up to check, again and again, but no one's dozing in midair. Must be the fan, or the plumbing, or the rhythmic low wave of cicadas. Or maybe your own breath, recalled in fitful turnings. When you do fall off you dream someone else's dreams, and wake not knowing where or who you are. In the bathroom, dark hands splash a foreign face—the eyes smudged, as if they'd been swimming underwater, away from some fast moving thing, glints of metal in its mouth. Meanwhile, an apple has appeared on the desk, next to the cheap stationary. You don't remember bringing an apple to the room. Famished, you take a bite. Sweetness in your mouth expands as the pieces diminish. That's better. That tastes like you.

THE ERRAND

Like an intelligence test for the weary,
these isle marquees—would Kleenex come under Paper Products,
or Cosmetics? Shortcut through Breakfast Cereals.
Pass a boy in a shopping cart jump seat, holding out
a silver 'Vette, thumb-sized. He's around three,
brown hair cut straight across his forehead,
still able to wander into a story by Grimm,
get lost between the forest and goodnight. *"This!,"* he says
of the car in his butter-roll fist. *"Yes!,"*
I answer, *"I know!"* You don't lose that boy language.
At the dairy case I'm struck dim by milk
light, and the miniature anxiety of American choice—
eleven varieties of shredded mozzarella. Settle on Wisconsin
All Natural Partial Low-Fat Semi-Dehydrated.
The teenage cashier is pretty, in that hopeless teenage
way, laying the receipt and change across my palm,
smiling like a dopey saint. Drop receipt,
walk out into dinner-hour hush. Cross the parking lot
past Skyline Chili. The bell for six-thirty mass
rings from St. James, and the early
fall light's beginning to thin: faint blue
smudges a fringe of trees. Take the back alley home.
There, a man I recognize from a Walker Evans photograph
jigs toward me, his body a rubber lure
spasmed ahead by transparent lines
rising from his head and left shoulder.
He tries to look at me, poor fuck, but his eyes and face
are locked in different directions. Fear
if he hits me up for change I will crumple
to brick, offer him my house, my car, my life. Our faces

turn from each other like opposite magnets.

Back home, late, as usual . . . My wife, who is also blameless, snatches the vacuum-sealed packet from my hand.

THE CLIMBERS

Poor men. On either side a green shield
angled against their ascent. The summit then
snagged in cloud. Or, the false drama
of clarity, senses free of obstruction—

Look, everyone, everywhere I turn, I see!
But poor Jesus had God's ear, curled
inside, and no need of height to hear, static-
free. He descended into desert.

Poor men. They climb like a column
of ants, lugging heartache on their backs
as if it were food. They set up camp
and a few freeze, a few return. But the danger

is minimal. Most stumble down,
throw knapsacks in the trunk, drive home—
What air, what views! Poor men. Poor Jesus,
blinking away the sun with his endless *No.*

EAST COAST POST-ADOLESCENT BLUES

Amtrak from above: a coastline zipper. Somewhere between salt marsh and the city, uncertain life. If there were lions hiding in marsh grass we would never have known. But there were not. *Hester Prynne embroiders her sin, all up and down the coastline* . . . The eyes rest comfortably on a horizon made of water, which explains the outrageous cost.

And I too wasted my twenties on the eastern seaboard, the dolphin revolving, always just out of reach. Church bells leave a steel blue residue on coastal waters. *What,* I kept asking, like a dog chained in a basement, *is life for?* Oh it's a long dismantling of that pose, assembled with hope and hard labor in the bathroom mirror, which for years enabled us to live.

THE PROPHET

Finally to come to a place where there is no one to speak for you because that is impossible, finally, and the shock of that snaps your head in a new direction where the mountains are inhospitable and the water tepid and undrinkable and your job then to praise it all anyway, or to find a chink in the stone where explosives might be inserted and a pass created where once was assumed forever the edge of livable space, and take your family through if possible but probably the opening will accommodate one only. And you go through absolutely unsure whether this is merely the last in an unbroken series of selfish acts your life comprises or whether the opening might benefit a few others in a way no one can articulate or easily turn to commerce, which god knows you would welcome since even though no one speaks for you *is* revelation both revelation and incontaminate speech have a hard road supporting themselves historically; generally a day job is required. So there you stand uninvited in that new place with words of your own devising shored up against your ruin, my son, which you are well aware has never worked for others so why think now, *you,* this time, etcetera, and in spite of that a weird happiness begins to gather your thoughts in a colorful bundle and behold, this landscape is poor but not without its charms and you take one, two, three steps toward a waterfall which seems to increase in height the nearer you come and maybe I *can* live here you think, maybe this kind of loneliness will not be so different from the other, and as you reach the foot of the waterfall where the plunging water boils up white and furious you begin again, removing one by one your aged and rent garments.

DAY ONE

Every so often some poet comes up with the idea to write a poem a day for a year. It's not enough that only around five people in America read poetry on a good day, this schlambaz decides he has to pester those five with bimonthly volumes of his own work. But what, I wonder, does this poem-a-day character do on the morning his father goes under the knife, say, for triple bypass? No problem—surgery's an excellent subject for a poem, even better when a family member's involved, all that built in emotion, etc. It'll be an easier poem day than most. And the day he gets the news from the Nobel Committee? The all expenses-paid trip to Sweden, the medal, the prize money, dinner with the king, his face on magazines, all the other cool stuff? No sweat: that day's poem will be on the transient nature of fame, how all we are and do is written on wind, on water. Yes, yes. I'm beginning to get the picture . . . If the world is perfectly indifferent when I write one poem, think of the exponential increases when I write a poem a day! I'll have to build an addition to my house just to store that perfect, enormous American yawn! Let's begin today, with the foregoing, calling it *Day One*. What a pleasant prospect the year ahead, now that each little calender square fills with glowing words, like advent windows. Yes, I'll do it . . . On second thought, I'd rather move to a small town in North Dakota under an assumed name, start a new family, and spend my remaining years making a difference in peoples' lives as an oral surgeon, oh beautiful, beautiful white coat . . .

ORIGINAL SIN

Fucking Eddie, walks out of his seventeenth rehab, middle of the night. Straight into some gin mill around the corner. Starts hammering them down. And it feels all right. You know that first half hour, a beautiful haze coming over you like glory. Yeah. Then real quick the good part's over and it's the same old, same old—nothing pouring into nothing. He don't know what he's doing, Eddie, walking out. How or where he is. You know. Falls asleep sitting down up against the building, out by the dumpster. Fucking cold night. I mean *cold.* Eddie's hands freeze to the pavement. Next morning he's still alive, but they have to amputate the hands. I seen him in the hospital. White stumps. I shit you not. And you might think, *Right,* this'll get his attention. Wrong. Whaddaya say, Eddie, I says. You gonna kick it now? Stay with the fucking program? Put the cork in the bottle, take the cotton out of your ears? You bet, Eddie says. Sure as shit. But then he says John, listen. It hurts like a bastard. Like a fucking bastard. I'm telling you—and here he looks at me, eyes all tearing up—I can't hardly see straight with the pain, he says. They don't give me enough. Can you help me out? John? Get me a little extra, just to get over the hump? It's killing me man I mean it. There's a cabinet right around the corner I notice they don't always lock. John, I'd get it myself, but . . . And here he holds up his white stumps and grins. Big, shit-eating grin. Fucking Eddie.

READING THE BAY

A calm water morning. After what was said on both sides.
Don't you talk to me that way. My daughter.
We cannot speak, now, nor stand to touch.

The bay, covered with tiny script
Moving rapidly right to left. Words
Crossing over
One another, whole passages
Torn from an asylum diary. I lifted her

Body, a huge flailing penknife, into the car.

A seagull sits bobbing on the text. My brother.
It appears that, today at least, all language moves out to sea.

BICYCLE, MARRIAGE

We take turns drafting each other so the hills are not impos-
sible and only half of us grinds it out half the time, each hard
minute bringing us one closer to relief. Of course neither of us
has died yet and that exercise may shoot our whole theory, but
meanwhile we amuse each other like Mother Beckett's boys,
Vladimir and Estragon, circling, changing gears beneath the
wintry tree, a music hall dog-and-pony-act. But we are not
brilliant enough for affairs, cannot imagine beyond what that
plot would do for the other—a fly landing

on the page of a novel you're reading and you snap the book
shut, splat. So that's out. *Sit down* we say impatiently when the
other is sick, because we are neither of us much for nursing:
Have a nice warm glass of Rilke milk. We have discovered and
recommend synesthesia as the elixir of renewable love: taste
her hand on his shoulder, see the color of his voice in her
dream. And yes, yes, yes: smell the children burning like leaves,
the sparks they throw rising in fierce wind, the loud ash of
their leaving.

MY NOVEL

Suddenly the eyes are train windows, passing towns weightless in speedy review. There's no time to recall who or what I might have known in one blurred city before another takes its place. And I'm seeing, after all, only the backside of things—weedy yards with rusted shopping carts, slant looks of smoking men on streets where all industry is of the human body. In the sleeping car with me, a crowd of men and women I've known— uncomfortable, flicking their eyes like nervous birds. A girl I used to love sits beside me. Her blue eyes are young, her hair pulled back tightly from her face. She looks afraid. The train car sways and the people of my life bump softly into each other, muttering apologies. I look away, back out the window, where night has turned the hedges, fences, rocks and broken glass a ragged, glittering black. I don't know how to begin. The city resembles the burnt edges of a manuscript barely saved from the fire. Ah, throw it back.

MY RETIREMENT

After the hail the humidity finally escaped. I decided to lay aside the problems of existence: Why are we born? How can light be both wave and particle? That kind of thing. For too long in the dampness I'd been hacking through such undergrowth, pausing only to read the best-selling story of Fermat's Last Theorem, which was spoiled in the end by my inability to understand the math, and therefore what was at stake. And what is at stake means everything, does it not? At least I said this, or something similar, each morning, as if lifting weights in my head. The haze made me forgot how much weather has to do with suicide.

At length, the sun's hammer quit, and each thing in the world regained its sharp edge. The ocean itself looked dry with original clarity. *Enough,* I said, and put the leather horse of my notebook back in its stall. Walked out in a breeze so adorable I continued walking, clean off the pier and, on slow legs, across the rocky bottom. Above my head passing hulls opened seams of light that flashed and faded, and I saw no meaning beyond that light and the sea, which I breathed in through spiffy new gills. Until the warm welcome I received, when I rose, streaming and triumphant, on the shore of the new world.

2. THEORIES & INVENTIONS

THEORY OF HEAVEN

Theory of heaven in which residents are permitted to time-travel as tourists among the living, stopping whenever they like and staying in one village for millennia, or choosing the many-cities tour. So that we are walking through not the stone angels of Venice or the sheep of Killarney, but groups of translucent tourists whose home base is heaven. Or, they are walking through us, living close by, and only the occasional feather touch tells them or us we are host to the other, which we sometimes call ghost.

INVENTION TO MAKE USE OF SKI SLOPES IN THE OFF SEASON

In which we line the mountain runs with flat but powerful magnets just beneath the surface. Then a station at mountain's peak where patrons are fitted with magnetic suits exactly calibrated to meet the buried magnets with equal force, so that, properly suited, a man dives off the mountain and flies down the slope some fifteen feet above the ground. Aerobatics would be possible. Some could even walk down the swift air, with the addition of magnetic soles. Weddings in mid-air. Flying paintball. Magnetic Flight as Olympic event. But all could partake on the beginner's slope, and man for the first time fly unimpeded, absent any sense of effort or assistance, the border between dream and waking erased, for the entire length of descent.

INVENTION FOR THE TABLE

Invention for the table in which the tablecloth is star-shaped, the apex of each triangle tucked in below the chin of diners. Such that each may lean back and eat at whatever angle he/she pleases, and food detritus not stain the blouse, etc., but dribble down toward the common table, and thereby increase both the pleasure and humility of all.

THEORY OF MOUNTAINS

Mountains defeat description because they will be largely un-changed after each writer's words have slipped under the sea or burned to ashes. Or, more commonly, lost through entropy, a slow combustion, atoms of each letter peeling off like microscopic jets to join new form. How many atoms per millennium doesn't matter, since all time is available. The mountains also disappear, but long after words . . . I include within this theory all images of mountains, from Fiji to Everest to Washington, oil or silver or electron—the likenesses we never tire of making, which the mountains also outlast. And they accomplish this not with arrogance but with tender indifference, sun burning off the fog each morning.

THEORY OF LAST MOMENTS

Father was not easy then, and tossed and moaned all night before the morning of his death. Earlier he had motored his chair into the Florida afternoon, and asked the gardener, "Do you think it's painful to die?" Maybe his intuition was jacked, and the question merely pertinent. There are so many end-time speculata: from the humbly anecdotal to full-costume drama, with plush furniture and language invented for the occasion. Here's my theory: When it comes to dying, nothing beats personal experience. If you want to moan and turn in damp sheets, moan and turn. You want a hand to hold, take a hand. You want prayer or blessing? Here's a prayer: *God bless and keep you.* It's easier with belief. But you may still want to scream. Go ahead and scream.

THEORY OF EVERYTHING

We could build a life-size model of the universe, but where would we put it? Let's describe it with numbers instead. Numbers are so much smaller and more portable and polite. Some are sweetly curved, others sour and prone to rust. But all numbers may be burnished to a high sheen. Odorless, colorless, a number theory of the universe weighs next to nothing. Some carry it around in their heads. Others give it to the kids to play with. It keeps getting smaller, and at the same time more accurate. Soon it will be tiny, and explain everything. Then, though we'll have to go on living our lives, most of what we say and think—our other theories—will be so much bullshit.

THEORY OF INSOMNIA

Dreams back up where the stream is blocked for whatever reason. What comes is lucid but unbidden: How that bartender looked at you thirty years ago when you ran out of money and begged a drink. How he held that look as he filled your glass. You discover there are no empty hours of night—each minute in fact is dense, expansive—the air itself might be folded and stacked in the closet. Shelves of books like lost friends whose problems bore you. Your own problem: how to let go of consciousness. What is death, divorce, illness, even drunkenness, to that? In the window you watch a giant hand hold the moon beneath the horizon, like a head beneath the waves. The ocean is pounding in your temples, pressing heavily against your back. And though you know this can't go on forever, it goes on forever.

INVENTION FOR CONTEMPORARY PACKAGING

A BOX like a microwave but tuned to the molecular vibration of thick, transparent polystyrene or whatever the material that encloses a simple pair of scissors, and so many useful things we may now not get to without deep cuts to the hands and forearms, such that the package is placed in the BOX and set to "polystyrene" or "styrofoam peanuts" or "CD encumbrances," perhaps a few other stubborn frequencies. Then the specific vibration would free the scissors or the music by loosening the offending molecules, which then join with the usual effulgence rising from our lives, and we could get on with the slightly less difficult day.

THEORY OF THE WOUNDED HEN

Simone Weil's mind leapt, from those few friends she had al-
lowed close enough to harm her, to the wounded hen attacked
by other animals in the yard. Such savagery was not evil, she
insisted—only mechanical. She forgave. As to real food she ate
what the poorest consumed during wartime, and thus drove
herself to her own "de-creation." This was mysterious, but
expected—at five she had allowed herself no more than the
amount of sugar rationed to each soldier. Her life fit snugly
between two wars. Still, the word *de-creation,* like a tack in the
shoe . . . What did the workers at the Renault plant make of
this Jewish-looking woman who prayed like a Catholic, and
lectured them on the Upanishads? How did she know the
mind of a wounded hen?

THEORY OF HOME

If home is house it knows more than we remember: *Playboy* under loose floor slats, the star-crack in Sheetrock, asterisk of a final passion. Those parties have departed. If idea, then home is all things remaining probable—psychokinesis, true love, penpals from Saturn. A gift-wrapped innocence, which everyone wishes to touch, wishes well. If home is land, you shall have your narrow shaft. If people, you shall go with them, wandering off like water. And so on.

But all along the suspicion that home is made of an entirely different substance. And you, with your drawer full of passports, good for this cosmos only.

THEORY OF BLOWBACK

Even needles can't be safely hidden in the past. The dictator eventually attends a garden party thrown by his victims. Charred and disarticulated bodies do their best to clean up, to welcome their honored guest, who must make small talk for eternity. Boating is pleasant, except for the faces of the dead that rise from the lake and keep rising, their features dissembling in the clouds.

Oh, you are every bit of the trouble you have caused.

You are anger dressed for work.

We cannot see the smallest grains of cause and effect. My mother for example has married my father so far in the future, his death means little. She talks to him and feeds him in every room of her house. And it will be a long, long time before they are children again, and nothing in the world has yet happened.

THEORY OF COOL

Miles, because the natural world was so much slower than his thought. Wrote a novel in four measures. Of late, fallen. Too cool to care. Dead cool. The swimmer, whose skin knows the quickest route through water. Switchblades from the wall and pulls ahead beneath the surface, a wavy shadow. The Chrysler building, gold bars, wolves, raptors. Anyone who can fly a plane, or kill with bare hands. Antithesis of humor, which depends upon sudden, precise collapses of cool. Close up magic. Ability to speak seven languages. Sing without accompaniment. Cool admonishes the uncool by mere existence. The tiger that gnawed on Roy. Thin young women. To wake up one morning, decided: you will have what you want. You are hungry, and the prey you hunt does not want to be caught. Think. Don't make any sudden moves. Be cool.

INVENTION TO WALK ON WATER

Shoes of exacting buoyancy, not for the sake of cheap miracle but, first, practicality: to get to the other side. In this the double gain of daily fare saved, and the exercise of walking to work—Brooklyn to Manhattan, for example—across the river. Thousands of workers walking on water in the blue and gold New York dawn, backpacked young picking through the crowd with splashes like little explosions, office workers with their briefcases, stepping methodically between small waves. There must be water walking lanes, of course, and stop lights for tug, barge, pleasure boat. But aqua-pedestrians would have the right of way. There would be the first person to walk across the English Channel. Then, the Atlantic. The first murder of a water walker. First woman to give birth on water. And the old shall shuffle slowly across the lake at evening, when the surface has leveled to a hush. And lovers on their way to the island, where no one can see their urgency, their feet sliding like hurried kisses, the moon's silver breaking to pieces in their wake.

3.

ELEGY WITH YELLOW BOAT

To Ann Byers

The inconsiderate gulls came early
each morning, crying like old hinges.
Tom had trouble sleeping. But you
slept soundly and when you woke
sat with coffee, stealing a little time
on the dock before the children
commenced their litany of need,
your two-handed grip tilting
the mug to your lips, your eyes
squinting happily in the brightness—
blue above translucent green.
Turn: calmly as I approach
with the camera, click: your skin pale
as the white mug, your black hair
lifted by wind to the brim
of your straw hat. Jack, bitten by
a horsefly (the infected wound
ballooned his arm until it seemed
the arm of an older, fatter child), played
a round of miniature golf,
his hand raised in the air as if
perpetually waiting to be called on.
This was long before any hint
of your illness. We all felt sad for Jack.
At night you and Tom and Sarah
drank wine while I, newly sober,
made do with cranberry juice
and soda water, all of us talking/
flirting/teasing on the glassed-in porch,
light comedy played against the sun's

hammy death-scene, neon-orange
and purple sinking down
behind Horseshoe Island. And
Tom, remember? looked like a giant
in the little yellow boat;
when he stood and tried to fix
the mast, thirty yards out
then swamped—Christ, we laughed!
And: picking cherries in the orchard
outside Fish Creek; the cherry-
pie-making-mess that filled the kitchen
with white dust; our children's voices
spiking off the bay's surface . . .
Ann, it's hard to talk to you
now. When I'm with your husband
and children your absence whelms,
I feel submerged, and *see* you
with my latent eyes
stroke Anna's hair, Jack's cheek.
You are someplace, sure.
And I don't mean that swarm
of atoms giving you form has found
other form, or will. I mean *woman*
we would recognize, a place
that is *a place*. Where
is it then . . . We took a sail
on the little yellow boat, you and I
one dusk when the water smoothed,
careful stepping in, pushing off,
so as not to follow Tom.
I don't remember what we said

though we must have joked—
your dry wit straight-man to my
absurdist bent. Or was it only that
I loved your laugh? I do remember
the wind was off and on
and we drifted, becalmed, watching
gulls wheel over Anderson's Dock,
small waves fold in beneath
the hull. Also, I remember our families'
impatience at our return, because
we'd kept dinner waiting: squalls broken
out among the children, meat overdone,
etc. All came right before sleep.
This is what I remember.
Now you have drifted out alone
and we are still on shore, if you'll
excuse the beaten metaphor.
But maybe you won't. Maybe
I should say you died and let it go
at that, the distance too far
for any language, common, or rare.
Besides, you knew the difference
between true feeling and sentimentality—
knew then and must know now
where you stand. But, listen: I'm glad you
have not left us, entirely.
I'm glad love is too enormous
to follow rules of time and space;
glad you can read this now without glasses.
And: I'll see you, when I see you.

THE SEVEN WONDERS OF MY ROOM

Spectroscope, made with Dad for the science fair. You point it at any light and the rainbow tells you what elements are burning. The dinosaurs come in cereal boxes. It's cereal I don't even like, but the dinosaurs I do. Except for the nightmares. This is a picture I drew. I think it's a naked lady. When my mother found it, I told her it was a kind of machine. She said that's ok, you can keep it. This is the switchblade I got off Frankie Miller. It's real. Don't even open it. Old time projector, from when Poppy was a kid. My cousins come over and I set it up in the closet and we have a show. The pictures are stupid but it's kind of cool, in the closet. My Red Skelton book. I like Red Skelton and every time there's an article on him I cut it out and put it in here. This is my Frankenstein. I made him out of clay and clear plastic tubing. I mix up red dye and inject it in his arm and it goes all around his body. That's what I want to do when I grow up, make monsters. I mean wonders.

THE SINGER

This morning I began with large ambition to write a love poem. Give me a sonnet, I prayed, that captures my longing for the beloved. After all, I *do* love, I'm sure of it. But as soon as I wrote one line I saw how instantly familiar it was: the words in an order they had known before, in someone else's life, from someone else's mouth. It wasn't mine. When I crossed that line out and tried to begin again, no words came. Instead, my mind filled with an image of Rosemary Clooney, singing "They Can't Take That Away from Me." I'd seen the clip on TV the night before, because Rosemary had just died, after a long and brilliant career that included—as they say in Hollywood—bouts of addiction and depression. Rosemary was huge, she looked like a circus tent with a head poking through the top. She was singing but, really, she was dead.

STY

A tiny itch in the far left corner of one eye. When I rub, the itch becomes a sliver, a pain of equal size. Look, while I have the chance: wind in the flags atop the schooner's canted masts, triangular ripples of red on white. The gull, not lifting a feather to hang there, still. Up the rise of the far shore the houses of the rich, the ink of expensive shadow spilled down lawns. Today the sea has stone blue eyes. The sky, mixed with cloud: white.

These and other pleasures of vision recede. My eye is shrinking. Soon it's as small as the money I have made in this life. I am the cyclops of early dreams, the waking world a band of postcards. Without the distraction of depth my head tilts—all the books I've ever read slide to one corner of my brain. Only love or salt water can unlock such an eye. And so I return to the sea: my eye a portal, a lure, a drain. Come water, rush into sand.

RUPERT MURDOCH'S YACHT

For Sue Ellen & Stuart

We passed her moored in Mystic harbor, one evening on the darkening side of dusk. In the curved glass of the aft cabin, lit like a yellow lozenge, young men with economical hair came and went. It took two minutes to glide her length, her name in retrospect: *NEWS.* We were in a small skiff, on the way back from picnicking near Mouse Island. The skiff belonged to our poet friend and her husband, the director of a maritime museum. Four sailors, eight hands of the non-profit school. We each felt the humility of these facts, I think, though we had the money of our demographic—luxury of the dead-center American average. But the future was stretched thin, retirement a blank spot looming, just ahead. What if parents had to be cared for? What if the children came back? Our minds failed? We did not want Sweden in Connecticut, and though the investment bankers that surround us *are* assholes, still they are human, made in God's likeness. To motor back to the slip, under modest running lights, without fear or begging, dark coming on. *Money is a kind of poetry,* Stevens said. But poetry is a poor sort of money. This is a poem about money.

MY GENERATION ABHORRED LIMITS

So it's pleasing to think of an infinite number
of alternate universes: branches of a tree diverging from one trunk,
all swaying greenly in their slightly varying prospects
on sun and wind and the daily traffic. But in fact
I did not accept the offer to sell airplane parts out of Chicago,
which would've made me a rich man. I did not
urge Elizabeth to keep the child. And you did not choose
the other poet with his hand on your knee
under a table the three of us shared. For love, you turned
down the gig in Chapel Hill. And when we look over
our shoulder now, the spaces we saw as open air
are occupied, each choice inscribed in matter,
pith to bundle scar: as it happened, once, for all time.

AMERICAN INTERSTATE

Guy on FM had drilled three holes in his skull, to relieve some of the enormous pressure. He explained how he did it—with mirrors and a medical textbook and sterilized instruments—in a calm, reasonable voice.

It is important, he said, to get the depth precisely right.

He was much happier now. The world no longer angered him. It was as if his thoughts had been released into blue sky and cleansed, then returned to him, emptied of their terrible weight.

The interviewer was polite, though a tiny sneer protruded from his questions, like a needle from the plush of an otherwise handsome carpet. Still, it seemed clear that the holes-in-his-head-guy had been to places the interviewer could not imagine and would never, ever find.

On the horizon a cloud growled in a low voice as the fifteen-story radio tower passed through its belly.

MY FATHER'S BRAIN

The brain jostled by the long carriage ride. The many meanings of the word "ride" converging in the womb. The brain the common cabbage of the gods, a meal unto itself.

A face twisting to accommodate the brain's decline. Sick from memory he took a walk in a new forest. But even there every tree reminded him of a previous tree, a name gouged in the bark.

My father, turning inside out. It is a long process. Exposure to air causes the brain to rust. A smug ignorance grows on the doctors' faces, a fungus. They shave, sink turns green.

I pray for a halt to the proceedings.

My father turning to stone. It is a long process. His legs are almost there, and his left arm. His eyes, whitening.

Soon we will wheel him to the pedestal in the park where he can join the chorus of birds and weather, free of all memory except the one carried by each of his children.

And what is that to trees, to stone?

THE EXPERIMENT

I sewed my father into a specially designed, handmade bear suit. He was indistinguishable from a real bear, and yet retained the necessary functions of a human. I also provided a GPS radio collar. Then I air-dropped him into a densely forested preserve. When I returned a year later I found he had mated with an Asian black bear. He and she and their two cubs lived a quiet life in a mountain cave.

After sharing a meal of berries and honey and wild piglets I asked to speak to my father in private. He led me on a path away from the cave to the edge of a cliff. *This view of surrounding mountains and rivers and forest is magnificent* . . . "Yes, it is," he said. "What, you can read minds now?" I said. "A small trick for a bear, as it turns out."

I thought this over for a moment; but it did not change my purpose. "Dad," I said, "it's time to go home. The experiment is over." He stared at me with his great, incongruous blue eyes and bear face, and said, "No." "Yes." "No." "Yes." *"NO!"* he said finally and swatted a nearby douglas fir with one paw. The tree flew several yards over my head and came to rest in the snow, dirt trickling from its upended roots.

"It's been good to see you," I said, and rose. "Same here," he said and also stood, "but I think it best if you didn't come back." I agreed, and held wide my arms for a goodbye embrace. I could hear and feel the cracking of my ribs, which I consoled myself would heal completely in time. "Don't tell your mother," he said. "In fact, tell her I've died." "Well, you are dead, aren't you?" "Yes," he said, and scampered up the path with surprising agility, on all fours.

HOMAGE TO POE

I cut my father into firewood. He made about a half cord, plus a small bundle of kindling. All through three winters he burned, not fast and pretty as birch, not long and smoky as oak, but steady, with light in exact proportion to the heat it gave off.

Years later: brutal winter. There was of course no more father for the fire. But I gathered our small family and, on our knees, we gave thanks for the unselfish gift he had once provided us in time of need. Then all went to bed save me, who stayed up per usual staring into a fire consuming some other manner of fuel.

From within the play of flames I was assailed by a small doubt: did my father really offer himself so freely? Was there not the distant, muffled memory of his objections, repressed until this very moment?

I plunged out of the house, onto the porch, the cold smack of night. Stars were there, oh yes—distant and many, their clean, granular fires. But not one answered *yes,* or *no.*

LUCKY DAY

On the drive to work today my car pulled to the left. I stopped at a Chevron and looked at the tires. No problem. I opened the hood. My father was there, curled around the manifold, bit of smoke rising from his oily blue suit. "Dad . . . what the hell?" I said. Without speaking he began laboriously to snake around to another position. When he had stopped moving he looked frozen in the aspect of someone who had fallen several stories to the street. "The car's fine now," he said, "Go. Don't be late for work." He was right: no more pull. Also, not a single pain in my body or mind. Plus, universe not yet contracting. Lucky, lucky day.

THE THREE TEMPTATIONS OF MY FATHER

In the three temptations of my father I am confused. Is my father different than The Father? Of course, must be. But who then is the son—me, or Jesus? And why is the father being tested instead of me?

When they speak, I know. "Remember 1956?" the devil asks, "When your children were still children, your wife prettier than June Christy, and you could high jump six feet?" "Yes, of course." "You can have that year back. Forever."

My father looks out across the Long Island Sound, blue green sea and the white sails tacking. "Can I smoke and drink again?" my father asks. "Absolutely," whispers the devil. *"Forever."*

In the long pause that follows I lean against the chair I hide behind and it squeaks and the devil whirls. My father says "Sorry, not interested," and begins to walk rapidly in my direction.

"Wait, I have two more offers!" the devil says but my father doesn't answer and when he gets to the squeaky chair I leap out and he scoops me up and slips me in his jacket pocket next to his fountain pen.

I hear the ding as the elevator doors open and close, and the devil's pleas fading above us. Dark, dark as I pull myself up on the satin border of the pocket, inhaling the not unpleasant mix of cigars and ink.

VICTOR F. ON HORSEBACK

We are loved, we are not; we are unloved, we are wholly loved.
I myself have mutilated flowers so long I need one of those
little thumbcaps worn by moneycounters. But what have the
doctors done to you that you wander the river's edge aston-
ished as if for the first time by wild iris, and the young girl
holding it, singing her song of nothing? What have I done to
you? That nothing song is sexy, god knows, and her voice too
has widened your eyes. But wait, my mismatched father, my
best I could do—wait and listen. Do not lift her above your
head for love, not just yet. Do not give her flower face to the
river. I'm coming.

SOME COLORS

It's raining, so night is black and silver. My father directs traffic at the side of the road, the site of the accident. As I slow in passing he lowers his wet face to my window. His eyes flash red and dark, blue, red and dark. "Go home," he says, "Live your life." I drive on. The exit sign is sky-blue, with starry white lettering. Connecticut again. In the front hall of our rented farmhouse, my daughters' yellow vinyl boots. They are bent, and so beautiful I know I will drink again.

THE ADIRONDACKS

"Look," my father says, placing his hand in the sky, "I got the moon between my thumb and forefinger!" We are in a clearing, forest to the right. The campfire grinds out its squeezebox tune. "Go to sleep." My eyes close down on a bed of stars. It is all so European. I can hardly wait for eggs scrambled in the open. The morning piss, wherever I please. The day of the bow, animal slipping through trees . . . I'm nearly asleep in fragrant needles. Then: yanked back by a scream, wide-eyed and up on one elbow; my father standing, sniffing the air. He picks up the axe and walks rapidly into the woods. Some thrashing, the low grunts of physical effort. Now I'm alone, and the night could not be more American.

MY FATHER FINDS WORK

There he is, punching tickets on the New Haven Line, handsome in his blue hat and uniform, swaying expertly in the aisle. "Station stop Mamaroneck, Mamaroneck is next." When he reaches me I hold up my ticket but he passes on, as if my seat were empty. "Old Greenwich is next, Old Greenwich." Somehow I know he will be fired if he does not punch all the tickets in his car, so I rise, and call out. But I might as well be talking to the window—he can't or will not see me. Back in my seat I take up Mishima's *Forbidden Colors*.

I can't concentrate . . . Have we entered overlapping realities, parts of which are simply invisible, one to the other? Have I been a good son? "Stamford is next, transfer to New Canaan. Station stop is Stamford." In the window a piece of the harbor, the masts with their clinking halyards—which I cannot hear—and the silver-green water I have loved all our lives together. Suddenly I remember that my business in New York was not completed. But the ticket in my hand is unused. I can return, for free.

BLACK OLIVES

I take my father for an interview with Jesus, who has rented temporary headquarters in a cave. My father is not very mobile, so I have to carry him in pieces, one piece at a time over the dusty heat of the stones. Jesus is there, sitting cross-legged on a rug, eating black olives.

My father laboriously reassembles himself in the silence. Suddenly Jesus is next to him, placing an olive on his lips. The olive glints wetly in the cave light. Then, I remember: olives are one of the foods my father hates. I look away, hoping he does not say something to insult Our Lord.

When I look back it's just me and dad. I manipulate his arms and legs, turn his creaky head 360 degrees. And, hell: he seems no better than before. But then I lift my father and he is light, light enough to carry in one piece, and the evening air has cooled the stones, and the scent of myrrh trails down from a gigantic moon.

THE HIATUS

I worked for my father, and I was late. I parked the car and began hurrying across an expanse of lawn toward the office building. Halfway there I was seized by the most powerful urge to defecate I had ever felt, and without pause took down my pants and relieved myself on the lawn. I felt instantly better. But, then what? I checked every one of my pockets but there was no Kleenex, nothing. The grass was too short and slick, and would not do. I took off my sport coat and used that, hoping against hope that it would not show. But of course it did. The next problem was deciding whether or not to wear the sport coat anyway. My father's office had a strict dress code: jacket and tie required at all times. What to do? Suddenly an inner voice admonished me: "Jeff, you can't go to work wearing a jacket with shit on it, and that's that." Grateful for this leadership, I threw the sport coat to the lawn and began lifting and buttoning my pants.

In the middle of zipping I looked up and noticed an old man and a very young boy watching me from around twenty feet away. I had no idea how long they had been there. They were silent and expressionless—*like the weather,* I thought–for, while of course there *was* weather, it seemed to make no sound at all, have no smell, no color: weather emptied of any qualities whatsoever. The old man and the boy . . . I looked at them as I finished tucking in my shirt and straightening my tie, and smiled very slightly. What else could I do? Of course I was embarrassed. But at least these were two people with little power in the world. They could do me no harm. I began running toward the office. When I looked back, once, the old man and the boy were standing together, holding hands, staring down at my shitty, crumpled jacket. "Obviously, the most important event of *their* day . . . ," I thought with contempt.

My father's office looked much the same as I remembered, except that the walls were canvas, like theatrical flats, with doors, windows, file cabinets, Rotary plaques, etc., painted on. But my father: my father was exactly the same.

"It's ten-twenty" he said. "Where have you been? Checking on accounts? Doing cold calls? Where's your jacket?"

The truth was I didn't know where I had been.

"I left it in the car." I said.

"What have you been doing?"

"I've . . . I've been writing a poem."

"Oh yeah? Let's have a look."

I rummaged in my briefcase, and managed to find a draft of a long, failed poem I intended to work one day into my career-making masterpiece. I handed the torn, coffee-stained wad of pages to my father. He uncapped his pen and began reading. "Ah ha!" he said almost immediately, "A cliché!" "No!" I said, "I don't allow . . ." But my father stopped me with a raised hand. "Quiet! Let me finish reading. In the meantime, why don't you go to your office and get some real work done. I'll call you when I'm ready."

I left his office but could not find mine. There were offices filled with young workers I didn't recognize and, further on, larger rooms with grass floors and nothing in them. I entered one of the latter and discovered that the room's fourth wall opened onto a meadow sloping gently down, and ending finally in the sheer drop of a cliff. There I sat, suddenly very tired, by a willow tree just on the cliff's edge. The sun was setting and I watched swallows dart in and out of the melding shadows of the cliff face. The sky was streaked with purple and almost neon-orange clouds and the air had the slightly moist softness of young skin. It was very peaceful. I knew then that I did not have to go back to the office that day, that I did not have to go back ever again in this life. I leaned my head against the willow's trunk, the enormous willow that overarched the canyon's mouth, and fell asleep. Once, apparently, there had been a river.

HARD LABOR

Such a long labor, my father's dying.
A long time to give birth to his own death.
The due date has passed, and still no sign of delivery.
Shriven muscles. Anvil head, impossible to lift

from the pillow. Nether end diapered and forlorn.
And yet his eyes open on new light
pushing across the ceiling each morning, and close
on newer darkness pushing that. For me too

it's work: giving birth to my father's death.
I'm out in the streets daily, asking for sympathy,
lugging my puppet theater. But what can anyone,
you know, do? Two songs rail in my heart:

"Do Not Go Gentle," and "Deliver Your Death."
What will this child look like, when it comes?
When the issue of my father's death is born, the body
cleansed? Will it have my eyes? Call me daddy?

ON DECK, LATE AT NIGHT

Sarah gone and me whining again, viz.: God, why can't you end the killing, and while you're at it make me happy, at least more than the player's percentage against the house, which seems my lot. And God answered Child, how many times do I have to tell you this, your favorite goodnight story?—I made the moon and stars and earth, the ocean you love and the mosquitoes you do not, and one day you'll discover how I did this and I will beam with prideful delight. Lastly I made you and placed you, precisely, so that time

and planets and microbes find their reflection in you and become thought and matter, indivisible. In this you resemble me. I have given you what I have, more I do not have. I set you down running on the earth, where you may add or subtract. You cannot change the total but you may add only, and never subtract. Or, the contrary. What part of this do you not understand? Heartbreaker, Whiner, Experiment Gone Wrong, Blood of My Blood, you, *You:* Come to me now for comfort. Be not afraid.

DARWIN'S MARATHON

Why should I want to return
to a time where even when I occupied that time
I wanted to go back to another time
more previous,
and so on, like my head in barbershop mirrors,
endlessly deferring to its own
earlier version. What is the use of nostalgia?

I'm not sure if the ant carrying a comrade
off the battlefield is taking him somewhere to be healed
or merely getting the dying out of the way.
I do know birds are incapable
of such care. One sees them everywhere—flying, singing, puffed up
in the rain—but the sight of a dead bird is rare. Perhaps they
        are composed
mostly of air, and the earth's deconstructionists

find them quick work. Maple seedlings, green dwarves
taken root in the shade of a mature canopy: they
can't compete, they won't make it.
So why this tree-nostalgia for the future?
If my wishes had such little hope I would garden
every dawn. Oh for a squad of vultures and insects
to dismantle our discarded selves!
I would pay for such recycling. Instead we are the only

animal to run trailing a single file
of all the *I's* we once were, so that when we plow into the wall
at the finish each runner behind slams his loose fitting frame
into us with a jolt, until we are all together again, at the end of
        time, and
fall heavy and complete to the pavement.

ACKNOWLEDGMENTS

American Poetry Review: "Night Reading," "My Generation Abhorred Limits," "Impatiens in Drought," "The Cook's Tale," "Many Worlds," "Day One," "White Dwarf," "Theory of Last Moments," "Theory of Everything," "Theory of the Wounded Hen," "Theory of Blowback"

The Breath of Parted Lips: "The Invalid"

Boulevard: "The Hiatus," "The Singer"

Hampden-Sydney Poetry Journal: "Sleeping in Strange Rooms"

The Iowa Review: "The Experiment," "Homage to Poe"

Kestrel: "Reading the Bay"

The Missouri Review: "The Three Temptations of My Father," "Lucky Day," "Black Olives," "The Adirondacks," My Father's Brain"

Open City: "The Errand"

The Paris Review: "Widow's Walk," "Darwin's Marathon"

Poetry: "The Colt"

Pool: "Letter to Pessoa"

Slate: "The Long Marriage"

Southeast Review: "Elegy with Yellow Boat," "Souvenirs," "Allegory with Clouds, Airplane and A Peach," "Modern Maturity," "East Coast Post Adolescent Blues"

The Southern Review: "Gulls"

Tin House: "Bicycle, Marriage," "Indecision"

West Branch: "The Climbers"

Yale Review: "My Dates"

The following poems were published in a limited editon chapbook titled *Mother Salt, Animal Dad* (January, 2005), chosen by C.K. Williams for The Center for Book Arts annual

Chapbook Contest: "Impatiens in Drought," "White Dwarf," "The Invalid," "The Experiment," "Homage to Poe," "Reading the Bay," "My Father's Brain," "Lucky Day," "The Three Temptations of My Father," "The Adirondacks," "Widow's Walk," "The Long Marriage," "East Coast Post-Adolescent Blues," "Gulls," "The Climbers," "My Dates."

CPSIA information can be obtained at www.ICGtesting.com
Printed in the USA
LVOW10s2250221015

459308LV00001B/7/P

9 781931 337250